Library of Congress Cataloging-in-Publication Data

Weber, Edie.
How to tie scarves / Edie Weber.
p.   cm.
Includes index.
ISBN 0-8069-9579-3
Data on file

English translation by Heidi Singer
Photography by Susa Kleeberg and Friedmann Rink
Drawings by Klaus Ohl

1 3 5 7 9 10 8 6 4 2

Published 1999 by Sterling Publishing Company, Inc.
387 Park Avenue South, New York, N.Y. 10016
Originally published and © 1998 by Falken Publishing
Company GmbH, Niedernhausen
under the title *Tücher und Schals perfekt binden*
English translation © 1999 by Sterling Publishing Company, Inc.
Distributed in Canada by Sterling Publishing
c/o Canadian Manda Group, One Atlantic Avenue, Suite 105
Toronto, Ontario, Canada M6K 3E7
Distributed in Great Britain and Europe by Cassell PLC
Wellington House, 125 Strand, London WC2R 0BB, England
Distributed in Australia by Capricorn Link (Australia) Pty Ltd.
P.O. Box 6651, Baulkham Hills, Business Centre, NSW 2153, Australia
Printed in Hong Kong
All rights reserved
Sterling ISBN 0-8069-9579-3

Contents

**Well tied,
you are halfway there . . .** 4

**Tying Techniques for
Square Scarves**

**Tying Techniques for
Oblong Scarves**

Well tied, you are halfway there . . .

Working for several years as a fashion consultant, I have dealt with a lot of silk scarves. Often, right after a color analysis, a client will ask, "Do I really have to change my wardrobe or is there another way to deal with unbecoming or unfashionable colors?"

Another method does exist: With the help of square and oblong scarves tied interestingly and in various ways, your existing wardrobe can be adjusted to accentuate colors that are in fashion and becoming to you with very little expense.

It is hard to imagine fashion without the accessories of kerchiefs and scarves.

They keep you warm on cooler days and in winter but, most of all, throughout the year they brighten your wardrobe. Scarves not only save you money, but they also make you less dependent on quickly changing trends in fashion.

Almost every woman owns at least some scarves, but they often sit unused in a drawer. Then, one day, you are standing in front of the mirror desperately trying to incorporate a scarf into your outfit. Nothing is staying in place, the knot looks anything but elegant—how do other people manage to drape their scarves so expertly?

It is an art that can be easily learned using the 24 techniques of tying introduced in this book.

Square and oblong scarves exist in a variety of designs: solid or multi-colored, checkered or striped, with a graphic or motif design. Many sizes and materials are available. The ideal size of scarf for the various techniques of tying is indicated in the descriptions.

Some techniques of tying require a brooch or a necklace. By incorporating necklaces you can add a very elegant flair. Here is a tip: To reach the needed length you can knot together several necklaces. There is also a large variety of scarf jewelry available that you can use with these tying techniques.

In order to keep artfully tied scarves in place, it is best to use some means of securing them, like brooches or clip-on earrings. If scarves are secured by means of brooches or pins, you should realize that

when they are pushed through the material they can leave small holes.

You will find recommendations for each tying technique showing which are best suited for various necklines. Let your imagination roam and personalize your little work of art by making small and large changes. You can create your own look, and—who knows?—perhaps you will develop a new knot. These 24 basic techniques of tying square and oblong scarves will give you the necessary foundation.

Edie Weber

Mister

1
Fold the scarf to form a triangle, so that the folded edge points upward. Roll the bottom point of the cloth up to form a ribbon about two inches wide. Drape the ribbon around your neck.

♦ For all fine materials
♦ Ideal size of scarf: 28 × 28 inches, 33 × 33 inches
♦ Accessory: Scarf ring
♦ Well suited for V-cuts and as an eye-catcher in the collar of a blouse

The ends should be the same length. Now pull both ends through a scarf ring. Push the ring up to your neck.

3
Continue to tug the end of the scarf that has been folded over, until the ring at the collar disappears behind the front end of the scarf.

2
Pull up one end of the scarf in front of the ring, tug it loosely through the loop at the neck, and draw it down behind.

4
Tuck the ends of the scarf under the collar. In addition, hold the ends in place with a brooch or secure them under your brassiere.

Pinwheel

- For all fine materials
- Ideal size of scarf: 28 × 28 inches, 33 × 33 inches
- Well suited for V-cuts and as an eye-catcher in the collar of a blouse

1
Lay the square scarf out flat. Pinch the scarf in the center, grab—pulling up slightly—and tie a small knot.

2
Turn the scarf around and fold it into a triangle so that the knot is inside the fold, invisible to the eye. Drape around your neck with the triangle pointing down in front.

Depending on the size of the scarf, either tie the ends at the nape of your neck or cross them. If long enough, bring the crossed ends around to the front, and tie them in between the triangles.

3
Tuck the scarf into your col-lar and then arrange it decoratively.

Turtleneck

- ◆ For all fine materials
- ◆ Ideal size of scarf: 28 × 28 inches, 33 × 33 inches
- ◆ Well suited for V-cuts, round collars that are close to the neck, blouses, or polo shirts

2
Firmly tie the two ends in front at your neck. Roll the long edge of the scarf off
your chin downward over the knot so that the knot becomes hidden.

1
Fold the square scarf to form a triangle. Hold the tips of the long edge, with the triangle pointing down. Position the middle of the long edge securely in place between your chin and lower lip.

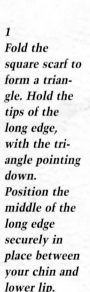

Wind the free ends around your neck, cross at the nape of your neck, and bring them over the scarf to the front.

3
Tuck the ends of the scarf under your collar and adjust.

Skirt

◆ For all fine materials
◆ Ideal size of scarf: 33 × 33 inches, 43 × 43 inches
◆ Accessory: Brooch
◆ Well suited for all round necklines that are close to the neck

1
Pleat the square scarf like an accordion so that a ribbon three to four inches wide results.

2
Drape the pleated scarf around your neck and tie it loosely by simply folding it over once.

Arrange the folds decoratively and fasten the scarf at the crossover with a brooch.

3
Should you want to wear the scarf on the side—as shown in our photograph—then secure the crossover of the scarf to the garment with the brooch.

Snake of Chains

♦ For all fine materials except chiffon or polyester
♦ Ideal size of scarf: 28 × 28, 33 × 33, 43 × 43 inches
♦ Accessory: Chain (approx. 30 to 40 inches)
♦ Well suited for all round necklines

1
Fold the square scarf to form a triangle with the ends of the long side pointing up and down. Starting at the point to the side, roll it to form a ribbon about two inches wide. Fold the top third of the ribbon back and forth to form pleats.

2
Take the pleated end and the chain in one hand. With your other hand pull the lower end of the scarf taut, and then swing the chain around the scarf.

3
Drape around your neck: the ends of the scarf should point to the front and be of equal length. Now slide the left end of the scarf through the right loop of the chain

and, similarly, place the right end of the scarf through the left loop of the chain.

4
Tie the ends of the scarf with an over-hand knot.

5
Position the knot on top of your shoulder and decoratively drape the ends of the scarf so that one end will fall to the front and the other to the back.

Crossing Point

- ◆ For all materials
- ◆ Ideal size of scarf: 33 × 33 inches
- ◆ Accessories: Brooch or clip-on earring
- ◆ Well suited for all round necklines and V-necks but also for blouses

1
Fold the scarf to form a triangle. Roll the point opposite the long edge to form a ribbon about two inches wide. Drape around your neck, and cross the ends of the scarf—they should be the same length—in front.

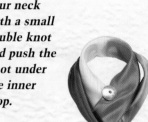

3
Tie the ends of the scarf at the nape of your neck with a small double knot and push the knot under the inner loop.

2
Wrap the ends of the scarf back and bring them to the nape of your neck.

Important: The crossed ends should not be twisted but should lie flat on top of the inner loop.

4
In front, tug the cloth in place and fasten the "cross point" with a brooch or clip-on earring.

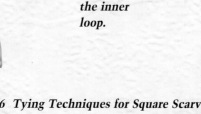

Autumn Crocus

- ◆ For all fine materials
- ◆ Ideal size of scarf: 33 × 33 inches
- ◆ Accessories : Brooch or scarf ring
- ◆ Well suited for all round necklines and V-cuts as well as collars of blouses

1
Fold the scarf to form a triangle. Roll the point opposite the long edge to form a ribbon about two inches wide. Drape around your neck.

The ends of the cloth should be the same length in the front. Pull both ends of the scarf through a brooch or a scarf ring.

2
Push the brooch or scarf ring up to the desired height. Bring the ends of the scarf back to the nape of your neck and knot them there. Hide the knot under the inner loop of the scarf.

Simple Bow

- ◆ For all materials
- ◆ Ideal size of scarf: 28 × 28 inches, 33 × 33 inches
- ◆ Well suited for all round necklines

1
Fold the scarf to form a triangle. Roll the point opposite the long edge to form a ribbon about two inches wide. Tie a simple loose knot in the middle. Important: Flatten the knot.

2
Drape the scarf around your neck in such a way that the knot is situated in front and close to your neck.

Bring the ends of the scarf behind to cross at the nape of your neck and around to the front . . .

3
. . . and from left to right and right to left slip the ends through the loose front knot.

4
*If needed,
tighten the
knot and dec-
oratively tug
apart the ends
of the scarf.*

Knotted Ring

◆ For all materials
◆ Ideal size of scarf: 33 × 33 inches
◆ Well suited for all round necklines

1
Fold the scarf to form a triangle. Roll the point opposite the long edge to form a ribbon about two inches wide. Drape the scarf around

your neck, letting one end hang down about six inches more than the other end. Tie a simple loose knot on the longer end at the height of your neck.

2
Position the knot below your larynx and bring its end around to the nape of your neck.

3
Now slip the second end through the knot behind the knotted end. Bring it also around to the back of your neck.

4
Tie the ends with a double knot and hide them under the scarf.

5 *The tied scarf should be positioned like a ring around your neck.*

Ring-Around-the-Rosy

◆ For all fine materials, including cotton

◆ Ideal size of scarf: 33 × 33 inches, 43 × 43 inches

◆ Accessories: Two scarf rings (or pendants)

◆ Well suited for all necklines; can also be used under collars of blouses

3
Hide the knot under the scarf. Slide the scarf rings in place and adjust the loops decoratively.

1
Fold the scarf to form a triangle. Roll the point opposite the long edge to form a ribbon about two inches wide. Drape around your neck in such a way

that the ends of the scarf are in front and of equal length. Pull on two scarf rings, one from the left and one from the right, and push them along to about the height of your bosom.

2
Below the scarf rings, simply cross the ends of the scarf and then bring them around to the nape of your neck. Tie a double knot.

Braided Chain

1
Fold the scarf to form a triangle. Roll the point opposite the long edge to form a ribbon about two inches wide. Wrap the ends of the scarf so that you have a loop. It should be wide enough

♦ For all materials
♦ Ideal size of scarf: 33 × 33 inches, 43 × 43 inches
♦ Accessory: Pearl necklace, about 32 inches long
♦ Well suited for all round necklines or as an eye-catcher over the collar of a blouse.

to pull over your head. Unclasp the pearl necklace, hang it from the loop, and refasten it.

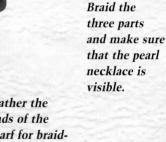

2
Gather the ends of the scarf for braiding. The necklace serves as a third strand in addition to the two ends of the scarf.

3
Braid the three parts and make sure that the pearl necklace is visible.

4

At their tips, separate the gathered ends of the cloth again, pull one end through the chain, and bring the other end around the braid. Knot both ends together and hide the ends under the cloth.

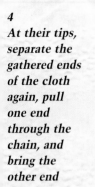

5

Pull the finished braided chain over your head so that the braided part is in the front.

Shoulder Array

- ◆ For all materials
- ◆ Ideal size of scarf: 33 × 33 inches, 43 × 43 inches
- ◆ Accessories: Brooch(es)
- ◆ Well suited as an eye-catcher on a simple dress or over blazers, jackets, coats

Carefully fasten the scarf with one large or two small brooches to your garment.

*2
With ends hanging down, drape the pleated cloth over your shoulder.*

*1
Fold the square scarf to form a triangle. Starting along the long edge, pleat to form a ribbon about four inches wide.*

3
Let the ends of the scarf hang down from your shoulder at the same length.

Nicky

- For all fine materials
- Ideal size of scarf: 21 × 21 inches, 24 × 24 inches
- Well suited for all cuts

1
Fold the scarf to form a triangle. Roll the point opposite the long edge to form a ribbon about two inches wide.

2
Double over about five inches of one end of the scarf. Tie a knot into the doubled-over cloth. You should have a very small loop.

3
Drape the scarf around your neck with the loop to the side. Pull the other end of the scarf twice through the loop, tighten, and let one point stick out.

Diagonals

- For all fine materials
- Ideal size of scarf: 21 × 21 inches, 24 X 24 inches
- Well suited for all cuts

1
Fold the square scarf in half, forming a rectangle. Slide the folded scarf at a slight angle.

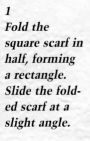

2
Lift up a corner of the folded rctangle and fold it along the diagonal so that you have two transposed triangles.

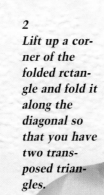

3
Tie the ends of the cloth twice close to your neck.

One triangle now points to the front and the other to the back.

Mixed Braid

◆ For all fine materials. Important: Both scarves should be made of the same material and harmonize in color; e.g., one solid-color scarf and one multicolored scarf.

◆ Ideal sizes of scarves: 28 × 28 inches and 33 × 33 inches—or 33 × 33 inches and 43 × 43 inches

◆ Accessory: Brooch

◆ Well suited for all round necklines

1
Fold the larger scarf to form a triangle and drape around your neck, over your shoulders.

One end should be 10 to 12 inches longer than the other. Near the collarbone tie a double knot around the longer end by using the shorter end.

2
Now fold the smaller scarf to form a triangle. Roll the point opposite the long edge to form a ribbon about two inches wide.

Pull the ribbon through the knot so that you have three ends about equal in length.

4
As shown in the photo, drape the braid across the front over the larger scarf. Bring it to the other side and fasten it with a brooch at the height of the collarbone. Hide the three ends of the cloth under the brooch.

3
Make a braid from the three ends, and then tie the three strands together.

Back Braid

◆ For all materials.
Important: Both scarves should be of the same material and harmonize in color; e.g., one solid-color scarf and one multicolored scarf.
◆ Ideal sizes of scarves: 28 × 28 inches and 33 × 33 inches—or 33 × 33 inches and 43 × 43 inches
◆ Well suited for deep-cut round necklines or deep-back décolletés.

1
Fold the larger scarf to form a triangle and drape around your shoulders with the point of the triangle behind you. The ends of the scarves which hang down in front should be equal in length.

Now fold the smaller scarf to form a triangle. Roll the point opposite the long edge to form a ribbon about two inches wide. Gather the two ends of the larger scarf into one hand to become one strand.

Bring the smaller scarf underneath it so that its loose ends hang down on the right and on the left, next to the gathered larger scarf's strand.

2
*Make a braid
from the three
strands, then
tie the ends
together. Turn
the braid
around to
your back.*

Flirt

◆ For all fine materials
◆ Ideal size of scarf: 18 ×
55/63/66/70 inches
◆ Well suited for all deeply
cut, round necklines

*Twist the
knotted ends
in opposite
directions to
form a simple
cord.*

**1
Tie a knot
into both ends
of the scarf.
Grab the scarf
by the ends
and stretch
your arms out
wide.**

**2
Depending on
its length,
wind the scarf
once or twice
loosely around
your neck.**

*To fasten,
twist the ends
of the scarf
around the
cord.*

3
Turn the scarf in such a way that the tied ends will be located at one side.

Woven Loop with Double Cord

- ◆ For all fine materials
- ◆ Ideal size of scarf: 18 × 66/70/75 inches
- ◆ Well suited for all necklines

1

Tie a knot into each end of the scarf. Grab the scarf at both ends, stretch your arms out wide, and twirl the ends in opposite directions.

Take the ends of the scarf in one hand and the scarf will twist by itself into a double cord.

2
Drape the double cord around your neck so that the loop of the cord rests at the height of your bosom.

Now, separate the knotted ends of the scarf slightly and pull them one at a time through the loop. Pull one end from below to above . . .

3
**. . . and the
second end
from above to
below. Wear
the ends of
the cord in
front or push**

*them onto
your shoulder.
If you do this
you must hold
the ends in
place with a
brooch.*

Simple Scarf Loop

- ◆ For all materials, including fine woolen scarves
- ◆ Ideal size of scarf: 18 × 52/59/63/70 inches
- ◆ Well suited for all necklines

1
Fold the scarf twice lengthwise and then fold it in half. Drape around your neck.

The loop of the scarf should be located above your bosom.

2
Pull both end of the scarves through the loop. All done.

Woven Loop

1
Fold the scarf twice length-wise and then fold it in half. Drape around your neck. The loop of the scarf should be located above your bosom.

◆ For all materials, including fine woolen scarves
◆ Ideal size of scarf: 18 × 59/63/66/70 inches
◆ Accessories: Brooch or clip-on earring
◆ Well suited for all necklines

3
Decoratively drape the scarf and embellish it with a brooch or clip-on earring.

2
Pull one end of the scarf through the loop from top to bottom, and the other end from bottom to top.

Crochet Stitch

- For all fine materials
- Ideal size of scarf: 18 × 66/70/75 inches or 33 × 75/79 inches
- Accessories: Brooch or scarf pin
- Well suited for all round necklines

1
Gather up the scarf and form an eye at one end.

2
From above, reach trough the eye and grab the long end of the scarf. Pull it through the eye to form a small loop.

3
With your thumb and middle finger hold the loop open from above, and again pull through the long end of the scarf to form another small loop—like a crochet stitch. Depending on the length of the scarf, repeat three to five times.

4
To finish, pull the end of the scarf entirely through the last loop.

5
Drape around your neck and tie the loose ends to the side. Fasten the scarf to the garment with a hidden brooch or scarf pin.

Scarf Bow

- ◆ For all fine materials
- ◆ Ideal size of scarf: 18 x 63/66/70/75 inches
- ◆ Well suited for all neck-lines

3
Fold one end of the scarf over the loop . . .

1
Fold the scarf twice (length-wise). Drape it loosely around your neck. The ends of the scarf should be the same length.

2
Important: The loop should be fair-ly loose around your neck. Cross the loose ends in front, below the loop.

4
. . . so that a simple over-hand knot is formed.

5
*Once more tie
the ends of
the scarf and
then decora-
tively pull
them apart.*

Cravat

- ◆ For all fine materials
- ◆ Ideal size of scarf: 17 × 55/60/63/66 inches
- ◆ Accessory: Necklace (30 to 40 inches)
- ◆ Well suited for all necklines

1
Fold the scarf twice lengthwise. Drape around your neck. One end of the scarf should be about two inches longer than the other.

Below your bosom, tie a simple, loose overhand knot in the longer end.

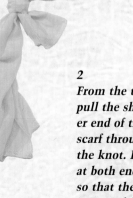

2
From the top, pull the shorter end of the scarf through the knot. Pull at both ends, so that they are equal in length.

3.
Hang the necklace around your neck and bring it, from the top, through the knot.

4
To finish, bring up the necklace in front of the knot, and then pull it down, again, through the knot.

Buttonhole Decoration

- For very fine fabrics
- Ideal size of scarf: 18 × 66/70/75 inches
- Well suited for all blazers and jackets with reverse lapels, round necklines, or V-cuts.

1 Gather up the scarf lengthwise and starting at the top, thread it through the buttonholes of the jacket. Alternative: Thread only through every other button-hole.

2 Drape the loose end of the scarf around your neck. Keep it in place with a simple knot at the end on the side where the buttons are.